Dear Ms. Redmond,

You truly are a gem.
Thank you for being
your wonderful self.

♡, Beau

To:

From:

A Teacher Gave Me Wings

Illustrated by Becky Kelly

Written by Patrick Regan

**Andrews McMeel
Publishing**

Kansas City

04 05 06 07 08 EPB 10 9 8 7 6 5 4 3 2 1

ISBN: 0-7407-4153-5

www.beckykelly.com

Illustrations by Becky Kelly
Design by Stephanie R. Farley
Edited by Polly Blair
Production by Elizabeth Nuelle

For my good friend Lee Ann.

-bk

show and tell

A Teacher Gave Me Wings

When I felt unsure and alone,
A teacher took my hand . . .

And eased my mind with gentle words
And helped me understand.

And when I learned to count and read,
A teacher smiled with pride . . .

And made me feel that I'd succeed
At anything I tried.

When I longed to see the world,
A teacher gave me wings . . .

And urged me always to explore
The in and out of things.

A teacher coaxed . . .
A teacher cared . . .

A teacher dreamed . . .
A teacher dared . . .

A teacher saw the path ahead
And helped me to prepare.

show and tell

A teacher sensed when I was lost
And helped me find my way . . .

And seemed to know the perfect words
To make me feel okay.

And if I lost my confidence
a teacher still believed . . .

And never gave me cause to doubt
my goals could be achieved.

The world is blessed with teachers,
but they're not all found in schools . . .

For a teacher can be anyone
Who heeds life's golden rules.

Wherever hearts are generous
And open minds abound;

Wherever there's a will to learn . . .
A teacher can be found.

No matter where my journey leads
I know I'll make it through,

thanks

'Cause teachers helped me be my best . . .
and my best teacher was you.

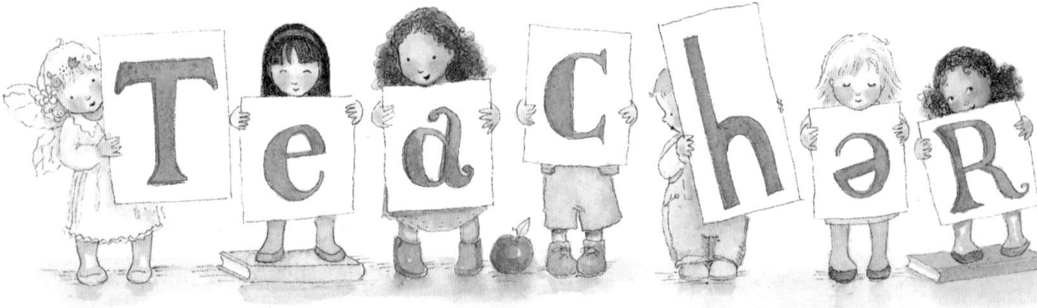
TeachəR